LILTING RHYTHMS IN HEART OF AN INTROVERT

ATI ANAND

This book is dedicated to my parents

and to you,the reader,with love.

Contents

Contents

1. DREAMS

Dreams that give you wings;
Dreams that give you sunbeam;
So like a stream full of stars,
Just chase your dreams.
Dreams that give you freedom;
Dreams that give you wisdom;
So like a real fighter, fight for your dreams.
Dreams that never allow you to sleep;
Dreams that make you feel alive;
So like a magician, alters your destiny and lives your
dreams.

2. THE ADVENTUROUS NIGHT

I went that night to another world;
It was adventurous and full of life,
It was like a dream, following the glint
Like those fairies, I was waiting for that twig;
Filling colors to those forlorn hope flowers,
Who brings back that charm and love in my life.
But suddenly the day has arisen, where I realized,
It was just a leaf from my book, who helped me to live such
a beautiful dream.

3. THE REALIZATION

I have that regret, why I never met him,
When I was counting one's chickens before they hatch,
But he made me realize his importance that day,
The day that I will never forget till my mortal,
Which told me a new way,
like a seeker and a butterfly, I was going in his way,
Then I found it was me who left him in another way,
But he always as a beauteous Halo circled round my way,
Everyone will get surprised when telling you his name,
He was none other than my failure, who was chasing me
from the very last days.

4. THE WINDOW:SYMBOL OF LIFE

She was watching everyone's move.
She was observing everyone's presence who was passing those roads.
Through that hope-giving lifeless window,
She was allowed to look around the surroundings and show her presence in this evil world.
Where she was dead deep inside but alive in physical form for all those passers-by;
Where no one even let her think to give her life a new start.
Where she can break that fetter and live her own independent life,
Where she was the only one who was impartial can think beyond her invisible bars.
And make each wish come true by taking some steps to those stairs,
Where that dream door was wide open to welcome her To go beyond that wall.

But before she could even think about her wisdom,
She took that last breath of her venom life that ends with
her own heartfelt words,
"Pardon for those people who were not aware of their evil
actions...
And have caged me in this hopeless place,
Because of saving that fourteen-year-old girl from
marriage,
And all I got in return was this lifeless room and with a
window.
A window, which was the only reason giving me some inner
powers to tackle this harsh situation,
Where even my parents were helpless to pull me out from
this world and break this door;
Where this was not an ordinary door,
Where keys can easily unlock that door;
But can only be opened,
when each individual is ready to turn their keys by their
wish;
Where that wall of thought doesn't matter to all".

5. THE SHOW MUST GO ON

The universe still exists as proof of our pure love;
When you left me with a child forever.
You left us and gone to a world; where I can see you only in
the form of those sparkling stars.
But this is your love which gives me the powers, that even
in those galaxies, I can recognize my that "one star"...
Whose glaze gets more and more every night.
Every night I talk to my star where our conversation gets
ends daily at one point.
Where my most precious star says, "THE SHOW MUST
GO ON";
That I always disobey.
But now it makes sense, for the precious one he had left
with me; "MY CHILD."

6. THE ETERNAL LONG DISTANCE OF SOULMATES

Honestly, I love the distance between us. Because of this distance, we feel connected by walking on the paths of our heartbeats.

Those were the golden days when we babble for extra hours.

There were times when we play hide and seek with our parents and luckily never get caught. Those days and their beautiful memories are still my only reason for happiness. Those days have eternally made an unforgettable imprint on my heart. But nowadays, my eyes often get replenished with tears; whenever I saw those portraits of ours.

Once, this long distance was the reason for our togetherness.

But now It has become the reason for our separation.

I still remember your last words when you said to me; that we are not that pairs pre-decided by God. Somewhere even my broken heart wants the same.

But at that time also, you were the reason behind my happiness.
Now also, your flashbacks and memories are the reason behind my little smile.

7. THE QUESTION OF A GIRL FROM HER GRAVEYARD

I ask you all, when will you give me; my piece of happiness?
When will you stop judging me by my clothes?
When will you stop horrifying me; with your evil eye?
When will you give me my piece of respect, which has always been dominated by you?
Please answer me, when will I be sure or stop thinking that any time, anywhere; the worst things can happen to me?
For how many years, I have to stand for my rights and self-respect?
Here's a girl ask you all to tell her mistakes,
Because she has lost her life because of your dirty thoughts in your head;
And that girl in the grave still, questions you when you all are, going to give her soul; a peaceful rest?

8. OUR REAL HEROES

Keeping that flame of fire in their hearts,
They move ahead to hash each enemy's head that came in
their paths.
As a lesson for all those people who ever raise their eyes to
look at our country,
And tried to destroy our nation and its unity,
For which our freedom fighters didn't even think once.
But today we, are in a worse situation, and here each one
of us is just pretending to be patriotic,
And inside, we all are afraid to be on that battleground.
Where we have to give our life for our nation,
And afraid to send our loved ones to be a part of the
journey.
Where our forefathers didn't even think once for all
acquisitive things;
Instead, they always feel proud that their life ended.
When they became the reason behind our freedom and as a
souvenir of sacrifice,
Want only, that flambeau of their sacrifice will ever keep
alive.

So we have reached a position where we have to take a
pledge,
Where we have to give our "real heroes"...
Our " soldiers" that respect.
Who acts as a shield for our country,
Where our enemies get tremble even when they take our
nation's name.
With that thought, to expunge our nation's name from our
world map.

9. RAIN:A SYMBOLISM OF PROMISE AND TRUE LOVE

Whenever it's raining, it reminds me of you.
Where we were dancing and making memories together,
Where the rain also became proof of our true love that we felt for each other,
Where each droplet of rain was like reciting our love story;
Where you, me, and this rain, have promised to be the forever partners till our ends.
It was you, who make a difference in my views,
To feel nature's beauty that lies in each part of this globe.
Where each part was on one side; but this was the beauty of the rain,
Which has made an imprint on my heart,
But all these things suddenly seem meaningless to me.
When you left me to fight on that battlefield,
Only to keep that pride and honor of our flag.
With a promise, "I will back very soon, set your eyes on that door,"

And still, it is the rain that is an inseparable symbol of our life, which gives me power and patience.
To sit on that door and keep waiting for that moment, when you will come back and cuddle me with your true love.

10. THE MENSTRUAL CYCLE

Whatever you call these Periods, Menstruation, Chums,
and Menses, all are the same.
But it occurs as a sign; that a girl is getting closer to her
puberty end;
Where most girls and women have to face this once a
month;
But she has been bound to feel ashamed;
Where her only shadow can talk about this part of the
menstrual cycle;
Limited to her washroom ends;
And having such backwardness and lack of education in
our nation's common man;
Each of our girls and women has to suffer a lot from this
unbearable pain.
But could you think?

....

....

If this menstrual cycle would stop in our females?

......

......

"Then you people couldn't even see that dawn."
So, there is a need to clear all those misunderstood
thoughts.
And try to open up all those negative knots.
Let's stand up by raising one pad.
Let's people understand;
Periods are matters of understanding and nothing bad;
Be the one to stop these perturbations,
And let this world know about what's menstruation.

11. MY LOVE TALE

I was waiting for you, till my last breath;
I was waiting for you, till my last hope;
It was me whose heart skipped a beat when I saw you;
It was me whose smile, especially matter those days;
Days which till hold my breath.
But even today, I don't know that mistake;
But somehow, it was the end of our love tale.

12. MUSIC:A PATHWAY TO OUR GOD

Music, a pathway of love where we can meet our God;
It is the rarest route to finding our purest soul.
It is the place where "I" also find my purest soul...
Where I find a unique world, where the rhythm plays the
role to communicate;
Where I don't feel alone since here, I find a new friend;
Who has promised to me; never leave my hand.
Here I find a new belief in myself and decided to give my
whole life to this pathway.
Here I can achieve every happiness, which has been
pre-destined for my pathways.

13. MOTHER: THE SELFLESS JOB

*"Mother," a word; that promptly brings a smile to her face
when her child learns to take her name...
"Mother," a word; that makes a woman get prepared for
that unbearable pain.
"Mother," a word, where all our pain gets vain...
"Mother," a word, we speak for the first and mention her,
in our ends...
She plays many roles but never complains.
We are the ones; who never try to understand her pain.
The "pain" which she had already left, when repeating
that seven vows along with her partner's hands and
promise to remain with him throughout for seven births.
And entered in that martial stage,
But we all forget those selfless efforts made by her to make
us feel well.
And in return, her expectations also get failed.
Now we all know that it's never too late,
So, give the mother that love and respect.
That's the only thing a selfless mother wants in her entire
life's phase.*

14. THE ENDLESS WORRIES OF BEING A GIRL

Why is a girl still being killed; before taking birth?
Why a girl has no right to see this world with her credulous eyes?
Why each an hour, her death rate gets increase?
Since we all are aware of being a girl is the reason for the generation to live.
So, why are we doing injustice and not giving her the chance to live?
Why are we establishing such an awful instance?
For those coming generations;
Who will feel remorseful when they will look at their forerunners and hated them for being such kind of human being?
Till we have the time to stop this horrible wrong deed and again illustrate the power of humanity;
To get spread in this beautiful world, which has always been the symbol of love and peace.

15. FRIENDS: THE PRECIOUS GEMS

They make you laugh even by their lame jokes,
They give you the strength to tackle any obstacles,
They are the precious gems that everyone wants to collect,
They are like the milestones that everyone wants to receive,
They are like a box, full of surprises,
Yes, you all have them in your life.
They are friends; who never give you a chance to forget them.

16. THE COOL CAPTAIN

We all get mesmerized and hopeful whenever we saw him;
We just get connected to his world, where there is no word
like being "HOPELESS" ever exists.
He is one of the reasons which makes our "INDIA" pride...
Which makes everyone; get inspired and love their life.
Everyone praises him for always being calm and being
focused on his work.
He is the one who makes our dreams come true;
By winning that gleaming World cup trophy,
He won our hearts too.
Yes, he is the nation's heart, having his lucky number "7"
on his jersey...
Known for his patent "helicopter shot"...
Yes, he's our " M.S.DHONI"...
Who shuts the mouth of every hater by his fours and sixes,
slays them on their home ground.

17. THE UNVOICED CREATURES

They remain unvoiced for an eternity of time.
But they never even whined in front of their creator,
Still, they were making their effort to be a part of our life.
The efforts remain only one-sided;
But they never even whimpered in front of their God.
They were digging into something, where they can only get
that heartless and stone inside.
But like an innocent child, they always hold our's fingers
and don't even think for a second, just ready to go
anywhere having hope in their eyes.
But each time we the "humans"...
As a swindler, break that faith and shattered their hearts.
Why does everything need to be a voice of themselves?
Why the beauty of silence; doesn't work for them?
Why an animal; is so helpless?
Why have they given a lot of attention only when they are
at the stage of extinction?

18. THE BACKBONE OF THE NATION

Where everyone's situation has changed,
Where we all are the witness of our nation's developing
phase.
Where we all are getting our basic requirements;
But that one whole community is still in the same phase.
Where they never crossed their poverty line.
And are always found compelled to take that poison;
But no one even thinks to mourn for a minute for them.
They are known as the backbone of our nation.
They are the farmers of our nation.
Whose livelihood depends on the nature of each climatic
change.
Where these climatic changes can bring happiness or
sadness to their face;
But we all are living in our new India.
Where we all are free to take a fresh start;
Where we all have to give our efforts,
To make the backbone of our nation more strong;
To make the farmers of our nation more stable and
happier.

19. JUST WALK ALONE...

If you want to achieve your goal,
Just walk alone.
If you have that belief in yourself,
Just walk alone.
If you have that courage to face each obstacle in your
pathways,
Just walk alone.
If you want to be an inspiration for others,
Just walk alone.
Walk alone;
The only way where you are the decision holder,
Where you have the power to change your destiny,
Which was always predestined by our family;
Where we were more focused on the word "impossible" in
our dictionary...
But never tried to have a look at the word "possible,"
which was also in that same dictionary;
And to make people believe in the word "possible"...
One has to walk alone on that path.

Where no one will look back, but always feel motivated to make another footprint on that path.

20. THAT UNHEARD VOICE

I always get astonished;
Where I found myself to be in that bizarre situation,
When that unheard voice gets echoed in my ears,
I always get stuck somewhere.
Where I found myself in some castle where I was left alone,
But still, I found that an unheard voice was there.
I always get tremble.
When I found myself near to an ocean, where I feel broken
when my sandcastle gets flow out each time,
But there also that unheard voice gets still echoed in my
ears.
But here I and that unheard voice has found that edge.
Where I found that an unheard voice was not unknown,
But it was my inner soul that always tried to awake me
before that precious time has passed away.
Now we stood with one another to fight against this evil
world,
Where humanity; has been killed but needed to be alive
again.

21. THE MEMORY LANE OF ALL

We all start our memory lane,
Which always brings that smile on our face;
Whenever we open that first page of our diary.
Where our precious memories of "school days" are kept.
Where we have done so many childhood miscreants,
Where we have learned the lesson of discipline,
Which still is needed to be stable on our life's race.
Where we were, previously taught "how to tackle with this
entire world,"
Where we do not feel ashamed while accepting our
mistakes,
Where we were not forced but to walk on that path of
honesty was our wish.
Where we have found those friends who are always with
us;
Even when we are, fighting against our bad days.
While we are reminiscing, we have that tears of joy in our
eyes,
It means we have reached the bottom of our diary,

Where we have to, again put that memory of our school
days,
Lock-in that diary and kept aside on our shelves.

• 28 •

22. THAT BALLOON SELLER...

The boy was going ahead in those thorny paths,
By keeping those dreams in his heart.
Where he had to throttle his childhood,
Only to run his forefather's livelihood.
And was forced to withstand this evil world,
Where he knew his propensity,
But has to bow himself in front of those rich people,
Who doesn't even knew the meaning of hard work, but
never stumble a moment to show off their powers;
That boy was always thinking of that moment,
Where he is an obstinacy child to buy that balloon from
his parents,
And giving his perfect shot for that portrait as a souvenir
of his childhood days;
Which he was going to have a look at it every day to get
those positive vibes,
But his imaginations never go too long;
And get him back to his real world where he was not the
buyer of his balloon's dreams,
But he was that balloon seller of his awful world.

23. MOON

When she gets to hide behind those clouds,
Then it seems that darkness has spread all around the sky.
From where, the wraith- silver disc moon appears like our
God, is giving us some blessings through his glaze rays of
lights.
But the beauty of the moon gets her part of the praise only
at night.
Which gets over when the dawn has come, and the sunrise
is ready to play its part.
Where we all begin our day with the worship of our dawn's
God,
But the moon's work remains the same to spread her shine
wherever she found that the darkness is to extinct that ray
of light.
But the beauty of the moon gets her part of the praise only
at night.

24. THE DEATHBED

There are three versions of every story, said earlier by all.
Your, mine, and the truth are those three said by them all.
Where the word "death" perfectly suits;
Since we all have different views on this word that makes
us feel apart;
Where some want, go to heaven when Thanatos, the God of
death is on his way to approach;
But their heart says, "I'm scared to go on that death bed.
Where I have to apart from my loved ones and can't
reverse my life to this route"...
But I ask you; why we felt so scared even think of being
near our death beds?
Where each one of us has to go,
Where our own decisions of living on this planet; have
been destined by our God.
Why we always want to avoid the truth?
"We, humans, are only a part of this journey...
Where each individual's unique identity make a special
place in someone's heart, wherever they met during their
journey, and lastly get back to those five elements of
nature,
From which our body has made.

And remain in ashes they are remembered forever and ever
in hearts of people they wherever have met."

25. THE SWING:MEMORIES OF CHILDHOOD

I love my childhood memories that were real but rare;
Where my parents also behave like a child and play with
me, with those uncountable toys.
Where there was only happiness and where our every day
ends with a laugh.
And the most precious part of my childhood days which is
still present on my ground;
That was the swing which my parents make a knot on those
Gulmohar's branches.
Where every evening, I spent my childhood life; watching
the magnificent views of the sunset.
Which always seems to be giving some life lessons;
I have the same impression and that emotional
connectivity with that swing, even today as a teenager.
And that swing will always remain as being my precious
memories of my childhood life.

A Message For My Lovely Readers

As the first step of everyone matters ;so do the end same. I need your all blessings and lots of love since this is my first move in this realm so more encouragement and love is needed to continue this journey to a long way.
Thank you all and wish me good luck.